D1497640

AUSTRALIA

 Treasure Island

AUSTRALIA

Treasure Island

First published in 1997 by
New Holland Publishers (Australia) Pty Ltd
Sydney • London • Cape Town

14 Aquatic Drive
Frenchs Forest, NSW 2086
Australia

24 Nutford Place
London W1H 6DQ
United Kingdom

80 McKenzie Street
Cape Town 8001
South Africa

Copyright © 1997 New Holland Publishers (Australia) Pty Ltd
Copyright © 1997 in text: Joel Nathan
Copyright © 1997 in photographs: photographers and/or their
agents as listed at right

Reprinted in 1998

All rights reserved. No part of this publication may be
reproduced, stored in a retrieval system or transmitted, in any
form or by any means, electronic, mechanical, photocopying,
recording or otherwise, without the prior written permission
of the publishers and copyright holders.

Reproduction by Unifoto (Pty) Ltd
Printed and bound in Malaysia by Times Offset (M) Sdn Bhd

ISBN 1 86436 279 0 (hardcover)
ISBN 1 86436 287 1 (softcover)

WRITER: Joel Nathan
PUBLISHING MANAGER: Mariëlle Renssen
COMMISSIONING MANAGER: Averill Chase
SENIOR DESIGNER: Trinity Fry
EDITORS: Joanne Holliman, Anouska Good
DTP CARTOGRAPHER: John Loubser
PICTURE RESEARCHER: Bronwyn Rennex

Copyright © in photographs **NHIL** (Shaen Adey) with the
exception of the following photographers and/or their agents:

NHIL: pp 28, 30, 31 (bottom), 34, 36, 40, 43, 61, 67 (top left), 70,
97 (bottom), 99, 114 (left & bottom right), 121 (top), 140 (top
right), 144; **NHIL** (Anthony Johnson): pp 4, 9 (top right), 13, 14
(bottom), 15 (top right), 19 (top), 21 (top), 37, 38–39, 42 (top),
49, 55 (top & bottom right), 58, 59 (bottom right), 71 (bottom),
75 (bottom left & right), 76–77, 90, 91 (top right), 96 (bottom
right), 100, 101 (top, centre & bottom), 102 (top right), 108, 110,
111, 112, 113 (top left & right, bottom left & right), 115, 122,
123, 124 (top & bottom), 125, 126 (bottom), 127, 132, 134, 135
(bottom), 136 (bottom), 137; **NHIL** (Nick Rains): pp 14 (top), 18
(bottom right), 21 (bottom), 22 (top), 26, 29, 32 (top), 35 (top &
bottom); compliments of **Peregrine Adventures**: p 140 (top left);
Martin Philbey/SPORT.The Library: p 114 (top right); **Rebecca
Saunders**: pp 48, 50–51; **Joe Shemesh**: pp 126 (top), 138.

NHIL = New Holland Image Library

HALF-TITLE PAGE *Sunset casts gold shadows across an
eerily shaped boab tree in north-west Australia.*
TITLE PAGE *Like mysterious sea creatures, the Twelve
Apostles stand guard off Victoria's coastline.*
LEFT *A gleaming globe of the world hangs in mid-air
outside Canberra's Art Gallery.*
OPPOSITE *Australia's best-loved images are Sydney's
Opera House and Harbour Bridge.*

CONTENTS

INTRODUCTION

S hould you be looking for an unforgettable adventure, full of surprises, head for the island that is unlike any other in the world – Australia. The icons most associated with this island continent are 'The Coat-Hanger', Sydney's Harbour Bridge; the sail-like canopies of Sydney Opera House; Alice Springs, the outback town immortalised by the novel and television series, *A Town Like Alice*; and the Great Barrier Reef, one of the seven wonders of the world. In addition to these celebrated images, the world's largest island and smallest continent contains a host of other treasures. All you need is a map, an open mind, and the curiosity to delve.

To give you some idea of the scale of this country, and to help you decide how much time to allocate to each treasure hunt, consider these basic facts: Australia lies south of the equator and is swept by both the Indian and Pacific oceans, by the warm, tropical seas of the north and the cold Southern Ocean in the south. From east to west this vast sun-soaked country extends for about 4025 kilometres; from north to south, 3700 kilometres.

Australia is a big country with a landmass of 7 682 292 square kilometres. It is the sixth-largest country in the world; almost as big as the USA (excluding Alaska), 33 times the size of the United Kingdom, and twice as large as India and Pakistan combined. Most of the centre and a large part of Western Australia is arid, desert country, while the coastal plains vary from the lush, tropical rainforests of Queensland to the humid, luxuriant wetlands of the Northern Territory; from the fertile wheat fields of New South Wales and Victoria to the emerald hills and tumbling rivers of Tasmania.

With a population of slightly over 18 million spread over such a large territory, the country's population density is one of the lowest in the world. Much of the interior is uninhabited, except for a few hardy people of the outback and some groups of Aborigines, the indigenous population whose

ABOVE Sydney embraces its shimmering harbour. The main link across the waterway from the leafy northern suburbs to the bustling city centre is the Bradfield Highway, which feeds traffic over the magnificent Sydney Harbour Bridge

OPPOSITE Many of Australia's concealed treasures are found at the end of adventurous tracks. South of Alice Springs are huge, red sand dunes, which mark the road to Chambers Pillar. Until the railway opened in the 1920s, the dunes served as a landmark for many inland trail-blazers.

ancestors are thought to have migrated to this ancient land over 40 000 years ago. More than 85 per cent of Australia's citizens live in the coastal cities, making the continent one of the most urbanised in the world.

Living in such relatively close proximity to each other may explain why Australians are among the friendliest people on earth. It could also be because Australia is the only nation to occupy an entire continent and, as it is an island that shares no borders with any other country, Australians have never had any real fear of strangers. Australians also disdain rank and status and regard everyone as equal. To understand this, one need only look to the beginnings of European settlement when British convicts were off-loaded at Sydney Cove in 1788. Cut off from the land of their birth, and with little chance of returning, those early colonists were compelled to withstand the harshest privations and the cruellest of treatments. Despite subsequent settlements made by enterprising landowners and by treasure hunters who poured in from many parts of the globe to find their fortunes during the gold rushes of the 1850s, it took over a century for the British colony to become a unified nation in 1901.

Today, the traditional links with Britain are still being questioned as the population actually descends from more than 150 nationalities. With 3.7 million residents born overseas – coming from either Asia, the Pacific Islands, Africa, the Middle East, Europe or America – and with recent legislation acknowledging that the many

groups of Aborigines were the original inhabitants of the continent, Australians are a truly multicultural society that is learning to embrace its diverse past in order to celebrate the present.

Australia is a land that offers the tourist many contrasts and surprises like few others. If it were possible to be in more than one place at the same time, you could ski the snowfields of the Australian Alps (some larger than Austria and Switzerland combined!); snorkel or scuba dive through the kaleidoscope of marine life in the warm, tropical waters of the world's largest aquatic park, the 2000 kilometre-long Great Barrier Reef; surf the sliding waves off world-famous beaches, such as Bells or Bondi; or gaze in awe at whales wallowing off the Great Australian Bight. Alternatively, you could sail your sloop among the over 70 tropical islands that make up the Whitsunday archipelago off the Queensland coast, or fossick for opals in the fascinating underground town of Coober Pedy in South Australia – or, instead, find your fortune at Jupiter's Casino on the Gold Coast.

If you're feeling adventurous, trek through Kakadu National Park in the tropical north and gain an insight into a culture that has survived for many thousands of years. The priceless rock paintings by the Aboriginal people have turned the cliffs of Kakadu into the world's oldest art gallery. You can climb Uluru (named Ayers Rock by European explorers), the world's largest monolith, which rises out of the burnished outback plain.

While in the north, go spotting for the fearsome salt-water crocodiles lurking in the lush, languid waters of the tidal South Alligator River, or travel to the far west and hop aboard a camel train ride across Cable Beach at exotic Broome, the pearl capital of Australia.

For a change of pace, sail in a hot-air balloon over Lake Burley Griffin in Canberra, the nation's capital, or meet the Snowy River cattlemen while horse riding among the towering peaks, granite boulders and tree-covered ridges of Victoria's high country.

To get in touch with nature, visit gentle bottlenose dolphins which come close to shore to be fed by hand in the clear waters at Monkey Mia, 800 kilometres north of Perth, or watch a charming parade of tiny fairy penguins waddling ashore like clockwork when the sun goes down on Phillip Island. As for the cherished gum-chewing koalas and the bounding kangaroos, they can be met at the many zoos and animal reserves or spotted in their natural habitat outside the cities.

There is so much to see, do and explore on this wide and wonderful island of treasures. To rediscover the history of European settlement, just wander through the winding lanes of The Rocks, Sydney's beautifully restored historic precinct. For the sheer spectacle of unmatched vistas, drive along the awesome coastal route of Victoria's Great Ocean Road. Like any hunt, look for clues, trust your instinct, and let yourself be open to the charms of this island continent.

ABOVE *Cape Tribulation in north Queensland is famed for its misty mountain tops, emerald tropical rainforests and reef-fringed beaches.*

OPPOSITE *Kangaroos are marsupials unique to Australia; the juveniles remain in their mother's pouch for about 36 weeks after birth.*

ABOVE *The Whitsunday Passage is a sailor's paradise; the calm water-way is protected by the Great Barrier Reef.*

LEFT *Uluru exudes an ethereal glow and has ancient origins that go back to the Dreamtime of the Aboriginal people of the region.*

Timor Sea

Melville Island
Bathurst Island
Gurig N.P.

DARWIN

Kakadu N.P.

Litchfield N.P.

Nitmiluk (Katherine Gorge) N.P.

Keep River N.P.

Arnher

Katherine

Drysdale River N.P.

Kimberley Region

Lake Argyle

Victoria

Daly Waters

INDIAN OCEAN

King Leopold Ranges

Durack Range

Purnululu (Bungle Bungle) N.P.

Gregory N.P.

Broome
Cable Beach

Geikie Gorge N.P.

Fitzroy

Halls Creek

Tanami Desert

Tennant Creek

Great Sandy Desert

NORTHERN

TERRITORY

Port Hedland
De Grey

Dampier

Millstream–Chichester N.P.

Chichester Range

Hamersley Range

Cape Range N.P.

Pilbara

Karijini N.P.

Rudall River N.P.

Lake Mackay

West MacDonnell N.P.

Alice Springs

Ashburton

Newman

Lake Disappointment

Gibson Desert

Little Sandy Desert

MacDonnell Range

Lake Neale

Kings Canyon

Finke Gorge N.P.

Chambers Pilla

Uluru–Katatjuta N.P.

Carnarvon

Kennedy Range

Katatjuta

Uluru (Ayers Rock)

Dirk Hartog Island

Murchison

WESTERN AUSTRALIA

Petermann Ranges

Monkey Mia
● **Hamelin Pool**

Lake Carnegie

Zuytdorp Cliffs

Kalbarri N.P. (Pinnacles)

SOUTH

Geraldton

Great Victoria Desert

Lake Barlee

Nambung N.P. →

Lake Moore

Kalgoorlie-Boulder

Nullarbor Plain

Nullarbor Reserve

Yellabinna Reserve

PERTH

Swan

Rottnest Island
Fremantle

Norseman
Lake Cowan

Nullarbor N.P.

Ceduna

Wave Rock ●

Leeuwin–Naturaliste N.P.

Stirling Range

Stirling Range N.P.

Esperance

Cape Arid N.P.

Nullarbor Cliffs

Margaret River

Manjimup

Fitzgerald River N.P.

Cape Le Grand N.P.

Walpole–Nornalup N.P.

Great Australian Bight

SOUTHERN OCEAN

A SAPPHIRE CITY
Sparkling Sydney

S ydney is a city on the move. Poised on the edge of Bennelong Point, the Opera House looks set to catch the breeze and head out to sea. An endless loop of traffic between the North Shore and the southern suburbs flows across the monumental Harbour Bridge. Massive ships, luxury liners, ferries and pleasure craft constantly churn the sparkling harbour waters.

The city was the site of the country's first European settlement in 1788, when the 11 tall ships of the First Fleet sailed into uncharted Port Jackson. Today, with a population of almost 3.8 million, Sydney is the largest and oldest city in the South Pacific.

The architecture of Sydney, capital of Australia's wealthiest state, New South Wales, is imposing. Sculpted, honey-coloured sandstone buildings – sometimes opulently florid – recall elegant days of yore. Grand arcades provide a showcase for local and imported merchandise. Towering contemporary super-structures highlight the city's international trade connections.

Sydneysiders love to play. Thousands of revellers will watch the start of the Sydney to Hobart Ocean Yacht Race on Boxing Day or the Ferry Boat Race on Australia Day. Others will flock to Taronga Zoo to marvel at its collection of animals from around the globe, as well as Australia's own koala, platypus and Tasmanian tiger. Some will dare to eyeball killer sharks in the country's largest underwater aquarium at Darling Harbour, or just stroll through the exquisite Chinese Garden.

Crowds are also drawn to the month-long Gay and Lesbian Mardi Gras, to street theatre at Circular Quay and the beckoning nightlife of colourful Kings Cross. On weekends and warm summer evenings, people flock to all of Sydney's 35 beaches, some of them offering the world's best surfing. And, as Sydney heads for the turn of the century, it plans to host the biggest party of them all, the 2000 Olympics.

ABOVE *A relaxing way to explore Sydney is aboard one of the ferries that criss-cross the harbour. Nestled beneath the towering skyscrapers is Circular Quay, the central terminal for all state-run and private boats.*

OPPOSITE
Located on the eastern head-land of Sydney Cove, the dramatic Sydney Opera House attracts theatregoers, opera lovers and tourists. Designed by the Danish architect, Jørn Utzon, the inspiring centrepiece of the harbour took 14 years to build and opened in 1973.

ABOVE *The great arch of the Harbour Bridge towers above The Rocks, the site of Sydney's first settlement, now a popular historical precinct.*

LEFT *The billowing, white sails of the Opera House and the sweep of the Harbour Bridge are the best-known images of Sydney. The bridge, built during the Depression and completed in 1932, was described at the time as 'an engineering wonder of its age'.*

ABOVE *New Year's Eve in Sydney is a time of magic as the bridge bursts into colour on a warm summer's evening.*

RIGHT *When night falls the harbour lights up, revealing the full strength of the bridge's steel arches.*

BELOW *With the first light of dawn, a golden touch awakens the city to a warm balmy day.*

PREVIOUS PAGES *Sydney has an incredible harbour. Full of coves and bays, the broad waterway extends inland for 20 kilometres.*

LEFT *The gold-topped Sydney Tower at Centrepoint Shopping Centre soars 305 metres into the sky, a vision of the 20th century. The ancient and mythic Apollo, Diana, Pan and the Minotaur are features of the ornate Archibald Fountain, nestled within Hyde Park.*

RIGHT *Once a derelict warehouse district, Darling Harbour now offers the very best in business, cultural, shopping and entertainment venues.*

OPPOSITE TOP *The sleek Darling Harbour monorail, seen here crossing the Pyrmont Bridge, links many of the attractions of this cosmopolitan city.*

RIGHT *The transparent tunnels at the spectacular Sydney Aquarium in Darling Harbour offer a peek beneath the sea, with close-up views of sharks, stingrays, coral and more than 350 fascinating varieties of marine life.*

BELOW *The idyllic Chinese Garden, a bicentennial gift from the Chinese Guangdong Province, provides a peaceful haven from the hustle and bustle of the city centre.*

ABOVE *The Queen Victoria Building was completely restored back to its elegant, Byzantine original, including its distinctive copper-domed roof. Behind its graceful, tall arches and stained-glass windows are many shops, boutiques and cafes.*

OPPOSITE *St Mary's Cathedral was the last Gothic cathedral built in the world and its magnificent peal of 14 bells is equalled only by Canterbury Cathedral in England.*

RIGHT *State Parliament House is one of many Macquarie Street buildings dating from the early colonial period.*

ABOVE *The thrill of the surf attracts many visitors to this sparkling city. Most of the beaches are patrolled by lifeguards, who often compete against each other in surf carnivals which test their skills and fitness.*

RIGHT *The sweeping curve of Sydney's most famous beach – Bondi – lies within two headlands, Ben Buckler and Mackenzies Point. Beyond MacKenzies Point is Bronte Beach.*

BELOW *Sun, sand and sea combine to make Coogee Beach the perfect place for a day of rest, relaxation and a swim in either the ocean or Wylie's Baths.*

ABOVE *Living on the fringe of the vast Pacific Ocean, Sydneysiders have an unabated passion for their harbour and everything that sails on it. The Festival of Sydney's Ferrython boat race each January attracts hundreds of spectator craft to cheer on the entrants.*

LEFT *On Australia Day tall ships with the wind in their sails salute the anchored 'sails' of the Sydney Opera House. Some of the ships are modelled on the vessels used to transport the first Europeans to Australia.*

BELOW *The Sydney Gay and Lesbian Mardi Gras started out as a political protest but is now one of the world's biggest street parades, attracting thousands of visitors each year. It is the finale of a month-long festival celebrating gay pride.*

OPPOSITE *The Royal National Park on the southern border of Sydney is an oasis of waterfalls, secluded pools, isolated beaches, craggy cliffs and rainforest pockets.*

LEFT *Palm Beach, the chic and beautiful seaside suburb that fronts both the ocean and Pittwater, is the most northerly of Sydney's long expanse of beaches.*

BELOW *At the northern edge of Sydney are many tempting retreats, including the sheltered beaches and maze of bays and inlets of Pittwater. On the western shore of Pittwater lies the largely untouched Ku-ring-gai Chase National Park, where over 180 species of birds make their home.*

BELOW *The trail across the narrow isthmus to Barrenjoey Head leads to the lighthouse perched where the Hawkesbury River enters the sea at Broken Bay. The Brisbane Water National Park, north of Broken Bay, is a trove of Aboriginal art and sensational springtime wildflower displays.*

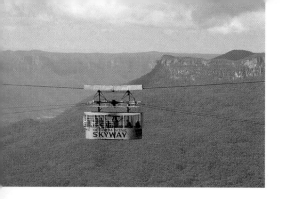

EXPLORER HIDEAWAYS

Blue Mountains, Jenolan Caves and Hunter Valley

For those seeking panoramas that dazzle, mysterious caves to explore and the tempting drink of the gods, Sydney is surrounded by attractions. Less than 100 kilometres west of the city rise the magnificent Blue Mountains. A little further on are the impressive Jenolan Caves. To the north is the wine-producing region of the Hunter Valley. The Blue Mountains are actually a sandstone plateau that has been dissected by rivers which have carved steep precipices that fall to the valleys below. Forming part of the Great Dividing Range, these hazy-blue mountains remained impenetrable to explorers until 1813, when the fertile western plains beyond were opened up for rural settlement.

Swaddled by indigenous vegetation, the region is home to over 100 species of birds and other native animals. Nankeen kestrels hover overhead, scanning for lizards and mice. Golden whistlers, sugar gliders and cockatoos flit between the trees. On winding tracks, accompanied by splashing water and the call of birds, you can walk from the Grose Valley and its soaring blue gum forest through woodlands of black ash and peppermint and over heath-covered escarpments.

Just 8 kilometres south-west of Katoomba are the Jenolan Caves, known to the local Aborigines as *Binoomea*, meaning 'dark holes in the hill'. More than 300 entrances lead to this magical world of underground rivers and glistening, fairy-like formations.

The rolling countryside of the Hunter Valley is where some of Australia's finest vineyards can be found. More than 57 wineries entice the crowds to sample and purchase some of the country's best-known wines. Bound in the north and south by national parks, the lush Hunter Valley is surrounded by magnificent rainforests, plunging rivers and steep gorges filled with Aboriginal art sites, a riot of bird and wildlife, and even a tunnel full of glow worms!

ABOVE *At an eagle's height, 200 metres above Cooks Crossing, the Scenic Skyway cable-car provides awesome views of Jamison Valley and the Katoomba Falls. It is the vapours from the forests of eucalypt that give the Blue Mountains their distinctive blue haze.*

OPPOSITE *The weathered sand-stone pillars of the Three Sisters are the most prominent landmarks within the Blue Mountains National Park. The enormous valleys and rocky escarpments of the region support a variety of plant species and wildlife.*

ABOVE *Numerous lookout points, scenic picnic areas and walking tracks provide panoramic views across the Blue Mountain's valleys.*

LEFT *The dramatic limestone formations of the Jenolan Caves create an air of intrigue, as do the names of the caves, such as Grand Arch, Devil's Coachhouse and Carlotta Arch.*

BELOW *The spectacular 300-metre-high Wentworth Falls tumble into the forest-clad Jamison Valley.*

RIGHT *Rhododendrons, which are actually plants native to Turkey, have taken to their adopted home of Blackheath in the Blue Mountains with great style and enthusiasm. Each year the region celebrates with a Rhododendron Festival.*

OPPOSITE *The garden at the Norman Lindsay Gallery in Springwood displays the sensual sculptures of the famous Australian artist and writer, Norman Lindsay (1879–1969). His life was depicted in the Australian film* Sirens.

BELOW *The Everglades Gardens in the charming Blue Mountains village of Leura feature an attractive pool, a cold-weather conservatory, and a distinctive variety of plants, providing a peaceful picnic area.*

BELOW *Browsing for something new or old in the many art and craft galleries of the quaint cafes, antique shops and boutiques of the Blue Mountains may unearth valuable bric-a-brac or an antique.*

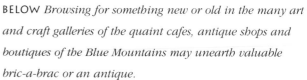

ABOVE *The Hunter Valley is the oldest commercial grape-growing region in Australia. An overnight stay will allow visitors to sample the vintages from over 50 vineyards.*

OPPOSITE *The red volcanic soils and sunny climate provide the perfect blend for growing the grapes which make award-winning wines.*

RIGHT *Many of the wineries in the Hunter Valley are family-owned businesses, and cellar-door wine-tasting is a must for any visitor.*

JEWELS OF THE SUN

Brisbane, the Gold Coast and Sunshine Coast

People wear life easily in south-east Queensland. Sunglasses, hats, cool dresses, lightweight suits and an ambling gait are what you'll need to uncover the charms of this sub-tropical paradise. Brisbane is a graceful city. Seven bridges link the banks of the city's broad, winding river. Glass skyscrapers overlook the waterway, Victorian terrace houses and Renaissance-style sandstone buildings. Bougainvillea spills over the latticed verandahs of timber houses built on stilts to provide natural air-conditioning.

Surrounded by lush, green hills, Brisbane is home to a widely acclaimed symphony orchestra, bustling jazz clubs, historic art museums, and the famous Woolloongabba ('The Gabba') cricket ground. It is the capital of Australia's second-largest state and the headquarters for vast mineral and agricultural resources, including gold, copper, lead, zinc, sugarcane, cotton, wool, beef, pineapples and bananas.

To the south lies the Gold Coast, 42 kilometres of contiguous resort towns and splendid surfing beaches. Within a sandal's throw of the surf, rows of high-rise condominiums, hotels, entertainment centres and restaurants attest to the area's popularity.

Less than an hour's drive away is the Lamington National Park, filled with hundreds of cascading waterfalls and densely forested valleys where crimson rosellas, satin bowerbirds and king parrots frolic.

The Sunshine Coast to the north has a different ambience. Fishermen troll rivers and lakes for bream, whiting and flathead, or head for the ocean to land black marlin, tuna and sailfish. Cooloola National Park, the enchanting Fraser Island – the world's largest sand island – and Noosa National Park present nature lovers with diverse habitats that are filled with bird, animal and plant life, swamplands, rainforests, wildflower-covered heaths, and huge sand dunes.

ABOVE *Vividly coloured rainbow lorikeets flock to the Currumbin Sanctuary on the Gold Coast to be fed in the evening. Elsewhere around the country, bird lovers hang seed-holders from branches in their gardens to attract these wild and prized birds.*

OPPOSITE *Elegant paddle steamers provide the best scenic views of Brisbane from the river. They dock at the Riverside Centre, where markets are held on Sundays, and stop at places like South Bank, a large parkland area with restaurants and shops on the site where Expo '88 was held.*

ABOVE *The broad Brisbane River winds around the city and meanders through Brisbane's suburbs on its way to Moreton Bay.*

LEFT *The Queensland Club (1880s) was built with high ceilings and open verandahs to accommodate Brisbane's tropical climate.*

OPPOSITE LEFT *Brisbane's 15-hectare Botanic Garden offers joggers and visitors views of the river and city skyline.*

OPPOSITE RIGHT *When the sun goes down the music starts; jazz, blues and big band tunes float through the air.*

ABOVE *Dreamworld on the Gold Coast is an adventure park with a difference; there are ten worlds of fun. One section, based on water themes, has the incredible Wipeout ride.*

LEFT *The beaches of Surfers Paradise and Coolangatta are popular holiday destinations for all sun-worshippers because of their broad sands, inviting sea and relaxed atmosphere.*

BELOW *A reconstructed old mining town is another section within Dreamworld. The Gold Coast also has more theme parks with fun rides, an IMAX theatre with a six-storey-high screen, shops, restaurants, an auto museum, a wildlife sanctuary and, for the energetic, jetskiing, parasailing, windsurfing and canoeing facilities.*

ABOVE *The sprawling Gold Coast region has grown around an extensive stretch of beautiful beaches.*

BELOW *Sanctuary Cove is a luxurious resort with its own stylish waterfront shopping village and marina.*

OPPOSITE *Lamington National Park, inland from the Gold Coast, offers a cool canopy of sub-tropical rainforest above the orchids, ferns, vines and mosses that grow in wild profusion. Famous for its birdlife, Lamington is also a haven for red-necked pademelons, a species of small wallaby.*

ABOVE *The Big Pineapple near Nambour is one of the Sunshine Coast's most popular attractions, especially the train tour through the pineapple and macadamia nut plantations.*

LEFT *Beerwah is one of the peaks of the Glasshouse Mountains – giant volcanic plugs that can reach over 300 metres in height. The mountains were named by Captain Cook because they reminded him of kilns near Yorkshire.*

ABOVE *Aboriginal mythology describes the creation of the coloured sands at Teewah in Cooloola National Park as the remains of a rainbow serpent that was brought to the ground by a boomerang.*

BELOW *The calm Noosa inlet, protected by the heads of the same name, is an area where you can quietly relax away from the nearby bustling tourist attractions and towns.*

OPPOSITE *Lake Boomanjin is one of over 40 lakes on Fraser Island, the largest sand island in the world. The Butchulla Aboriginal people, who had lived on the island for about 30 000 years, called it K'gari, meaning 'paradise'. The island is World Heritage-listed.*

ABOVE & BELOW *Fraser Island has a unique combination of rainforests, freshwater lakes and streams. It also has wide beaches, huge sand dunes and more than 240 different birds. One of the island's landmarks is the wreck of the Maheno, still lying where it was grounded by a cyclone in 1935.*

TROPICAL ADVENTURES

The Great Barrier Reef and North Queensland

Reputedly visible from the moon, the Great Barrier Reef covers an enormous 215 000 square kilometres and stretches for over 2000 kilometres. It is the world's largest living structure, and a diverse industry has grown to cater for the visitors who flock to see the magical underwater world, the nearby rainforests, the tablelands and the islands.

Amid the crystal-clear waters are over 2600 separate reefs, almost 1500 varieties of fish and around 350 types of coral. Extravagantly coloured coral, stingrays, sea turtles and an endless parade of tropical fish vie for the attention of the curious human faces pressed against diving masks and glass-bottomed boats. Many of the reef's islands are densely forested, edged with rocky headlands and steep cliffs, and often fringed with coral reefs. Just walk to the water's edge and you'll see the reef, watch turtles toiling ashore to lay their eggs or spot humpback whales heading south.

The gateway to Australia's greatest natural treasure is Cairns, nestling in the fold of Trinity Bay. Cairns came into being as a produce port for the coastal plain and the fertile Atherton Tableland. The lure of deep-sea fishing, the region's balmy beauty and some 300 tropical islands paved the way for the cosmopolitan, modern city it has become, with its wide streets, markets and restaurants. Parts of the city are reminiscent of the colonial past with white timber homes built on stilts to catch the cooling breezes, gardens of bougainvilleas, poinciana, hibiscus and palm trees.

North of Port Douglas are the Daintree and Cape Tribulation national parks, comprising the oldest continuously surviving rainforest on earth – more than 100 million years old – with the highest concentration of primitive, flowering plants in the world. A cruise along the Daintree River will reveal many unique Australian animals, like the rare cassowary, crocodiles, ring-tailed possums and tree-climbing kangaroos.

ABOVE The coral gardens of the Great Barrier Reef are home to many tropical fish, dolphins, turtles, humpback whales and gentle dugongs. Coral is formed by tiny organisms which secrete lime to build their habitat. Live coral is full of colour, but coral skeletons turn white.

OPPOSITE Green Island, 27 kilometres from Cairns, is the most popular of the lush northern islands on the Barrier Reef. Unlike the hilly, continental islands closer to shore, Green Island is a coral cay which has developed vegetation atop its base.

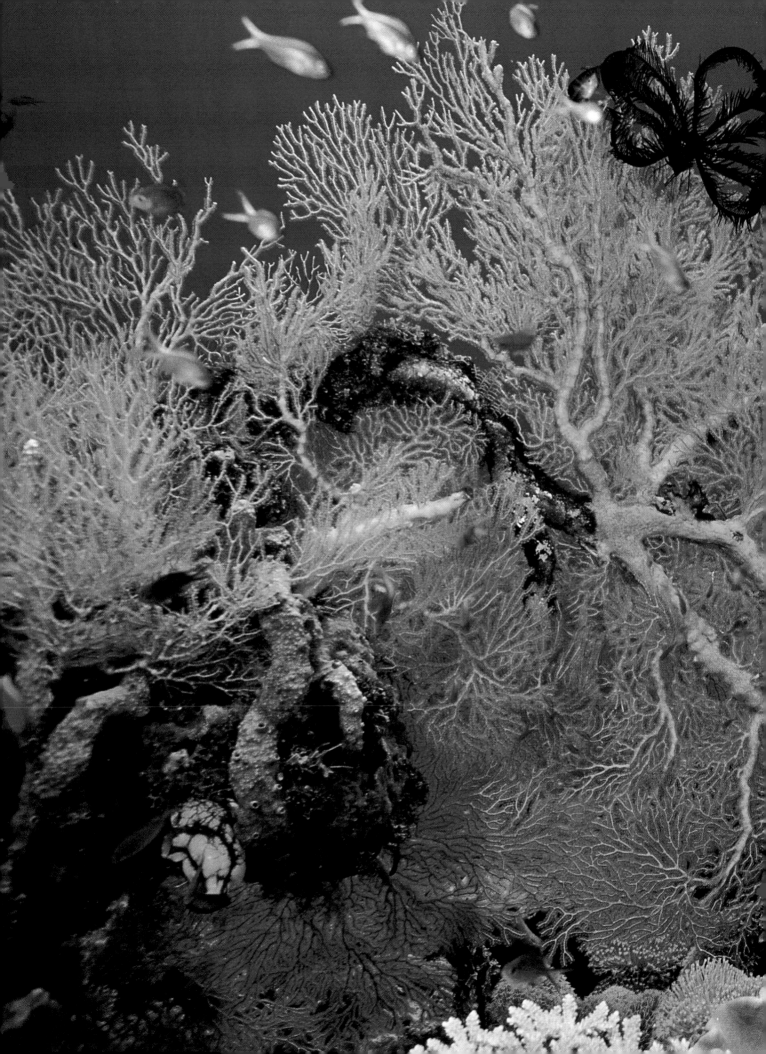

PREVIOUS PAGES *The magical underwater gardens of the reef can easily be explored by scuba divers.*

ABOVE *The harbour at Cairns, the 'capital' of Far North Queensland, provides a springboard for cruises to the reef.*

BELOW *The Crystal Caves at Atherton give children and adults alike the opportunity to explore the underground world through educational tours.*

OPPOSITE *The 100-year-old Kuranda Scenic Railway steam train winds its way from Cairns up the plateau to the table-lands through unspoilt rainforests, lakes, waterfalls and extinct volcanoes.*

BELOW *The multi-award-winning Tjapukai Dance Theatre troupe takes you back to the Dreamtime. The stories and cultural events of the local indigenous people are regularly performed at the Tjapukai Cultural Theme Park.*

ABOVE *Under a rainforest canopy, Mossman Gorge is surrounded by refreshing swimming holes and waterfalls.*

OPPOSITE *Like a pirate's ship, the replica of Captain Cook's Endeavour rests silhouetted against the evening sky.*

RIGHT *Cape Tribulation and Daintree national parks have wonderful walking tracks which allow passage through the precious and fragile rainforests.*

BELOW *The flowing roots of the ancient, 50-metre-high Curtain Fig Tree show nature's ability to adapt to the elements.*

RIGHT *Hoop pine outcrops along coastal cliffs and headlands, sparkling beaches and a coral reef attract wildlife enthusiasts, beachcombers, snorkellers and fishermen to fabulous Magnetic Island.*

OPPOSITE *Magnetic Island offers superb holiday facilities; tents pitched along the embankment allow even the most budget-conscious backpacker to enjoy the tranquil, laid-back atmosphere.*

BELOW *Panoramic views of Townsville, the mainland's best access point to Magnetic Island, can be seen from Castle Hill. The views extend across Cleveland Bay to the island.*

BELOW *Wallabies, possums, koalas and birds occupy the eucalypt forests and rocky headlands of Magnetic Island, named by Captain Cook after his compass went awry.*

OPPOSITE *Hamilton Island, 16 kilometres from Shute Harbour, has a 200-boat marina, an airport, bars, nine restaurants, and accommodation for 2000 people ranging from penthouses to Polynesian-style 'bures'.*

BELOW *For thrill-seekers, an aerial view from a hang-glider over Rex Lookout near Ellis Beach is the only way to enjoy the sights.*

ABOVE & BELOW *The Whitsundays are a chain of 74, mostly uninhabited, tropical islands. Their calm waters, expansive white beaches and forest-covered hills provide unending pleasure to snorkellers, campers, fishermen and birdwatchers.*

DREAMTIME TREASURES

Kakadu National Park

East of Darwin, the capital of the Northern Territory, lies the World Heritage-listed Kakadu National Park which was named after the Gagadju Aborigines, the park's custodians. Stretching from the tablelands of Arnhem Land to the coast of Van Diemen Gulf in the north, and almost as far as Nitmiluk (Katherine Gorge) National Park in the south, Kakadu comprises 20 000 square kilometres – an area almost as large as Wales in the United Kingdom. It is also unique in that it encompasses the entire river catchment system of the South Alligator River.

Kakadu is a place of great natural beauty and scenery. Saltwater swamps, wetlands, rainforests, waterfalls and sandstone escarpments provide the habitat for more than 50 species of mammal, 280 varieties of bird, 123 types of reptile, 10 000 species of insect and 77 kinds of freshwater fish.

The variety of life is as astonishing as it is stunning. There are hooded parrots and white-throated grass wrens, giant cave geckos and predatory saltwater crocodiles, sugar gliders and bats, ring-tailed possums and short-eared wallabies. The lagoons and billabongs teem with fish and attract spectacular flocks of herons, egrets, pelicans and waterlily-strutting jacanas.

Sheltered ravines with cascading waterfalls are filled with orchids, ferns, lichens and mosses. Combined with aromatic samphire plants, eucalypt forests and mangroves, Kakadu is one of the richest woodland habitats in Australia. The Darwin stringybark is prized by the Aborigines for the construction of traditional shelters and as a canvas for bark paintings.

With more than 5000 art and archaeological sites, Kakadu is the biggest art gallery in the world. In caves and on cliffs, thousands of years of Aboriginal history are reflected in the stick, realistic, dot and 'X-ray' paintings of Dreamtime creation beings and their stories as well as hunting, fighting and other social activities.

ABOVE *Ubirr Rock is one of the most accessible and well-preserved Aboriginal rock-art galleries. Aboriginal stories relate that the Rainbow Serpent, while on her way to visiting sacred sites, painted her image on the rock's face.*

OPPOSITE *Twin Falls, together with Jim Jim Falls, are among the most spectacular cascades at Kakadu. Pouring down from the Arnhem Land escarpment into a large waterhole, Twin Falls create a refreshing oasis.*

ABOVE *At the base of Nourlangie Rock are depictions of the lifestyle and culture of the local Aboriginal people.*

OPPOSITE *The Lightning Man, known as Namarrkon, is an example of the 'X-ray' art on Nourlangie Rock.*

RIGHT *Warradjan Cultural Centre near Yellow Waters displays traditional work by local artists and also stages performances of tribal dances.*

FOLLOWING PAGES *The best way to enjoy the incredible Yellow Waters billabong is on a cruise.*

ABOVE *Termite mounds represent the most ancient type of organised community on earth. Hundreds of thousands of insects live in these colonies and hooded parrots nest in many of their abandoned homes.*

LEFT *Yellow Waters becomes part of the Jim Jim Creek during the wet season. In the dry, the floodplains still sustain fish, wildlife and flocks of indigenous and migrating birds.*

BELOW *Among the beautiful plant life that flourishes at Yellow Waters is the delicate waterlily.*

ABOVE *The animal life at Kakadu ranges from the very dangerous to the very beautiful. The saltwater, or estuarine, crocodile grows to seven metres in length and can be fast, ferocious and dangerous.*

RIGHT *The jabiru, a black-necked stork, lives in river pools, tidal floodplains and swamps. With a 200-centimetre wingspan, its soaring flight is very distinctive.*

BELOW *Kakadu is renowned for its many reptiles, including a variety of goannas, snakes and lizards.*

RED HOT ROCKS

Uluru, Katatjuta and the Devils Marbles

One of the most memorable images of Australia is the red hot centre. Kings Canyon, Chambers Pillar, Alice Springs, and three distinct rock forms – Uluru, Katatjuta and the Devils Marbles – stand out in a landscape that dates back to a time before humans. Uluru, sculpted by the earth's movements and wind, is rich with the spirit of the Anangu Aborigines who have lived in the region for at least 30 000 years. Called Ayers Rock by the Europeans, its size is what takes most visitors by surprise. It is 348 metres high, 3.1 kilometres from east to west, 1.9 kilometres north to south and has a 9.4-kilometre circumference. Composed of sandstone, it is only the tip of a seam of sedimentary rock believed to run for several kilometres underground. Sheltered caves and overhangs have provided a canvas for generations of Aboriginal artists who have lived in this 'Dali-esque' landscape.

The same sense of sacredness can be felt at Katatjuta, 36 kilometres east. Katatjuta, meaning 'many heads' in the local Aboriginal dialect, is sometimes still called the Olgas. The huge dome formations consist of over 30 towering, rounded rocks that rise up to 546 metres.

The heart of the centre is Alice Springs. No other town in Australia quite captures the image of the outback like 'the Alice', named after the wife of the original superintendent of the 1870s Overland Telegraph Line repeater station. It is home to the Royal Australian Flying Doctor Service, a supply centre for far-reaching cattle stations, and the site of the School of the Air for children scattered over a region two-thirds the size of Texas.

To the north, near Tennant Creek, are massive granite boulders known as the Devils Marbles, which seem to have been deliberately piled upon one another. Originally a single rocky outcrop, the 'marbles' are evidence of the massive erosive powers of nature in the Australian outback.

ABOVE *The striking, sheer walls of Kings Canyon plunge 270 metres to a botanical wonderland that has been inhabited by the Aboriginal Luritja people for at least 22 000 years. Within the canyon are waterholes surrounded by verdant vegetation, called the 'Garden of Eden'.*

OPPOSITE *Chambers Pillar is known by the local Aboriginal people as Itirkawara, a creation being 'superman', banished for marrying a girl from another kin group. He was turned into a pillar of sandstone and she became the low hill that lies 500 metres away.*

ABOVE *A librarian reads to the children of the Amoonguna community near Alice Springs. But, for many children of the outback the only link with a teacher is via a microphone.*

LEFT *A cairn marks the spot of the waterhole originally named Alice Springs. The town began in the 1870s as an important centre for the Overland Telegraph Line.*

BELOW *The Royal Flying Doctor Service is honoured at the Technology, Transport and Communications Museum.*

ABOVE & BELOW *The Devils Marbles are located 104 kilometres south of Tennant Creek and lie in a shallow valley. Many of these seemingly haphazardly strewn and piled-up granite boulders are almost perfect spheres. According to Aboriginal legend, these rocks are the eggs laid by the Rainbow Serpent, named Kurangali, who represents the spirit of the land. Iron deposits upon the rocks' surfaces cause their famous eerie glow at sunset.*

RIGHT & OPPOSITE BOTTOM *Few other natural features attract more pilgrims than Uluru. For the visitor its mystique lies in its size and the way it changes colour from glowing red to ethereal blues, pinks and browns. Uluru is a sacred Aboriginal site and legend claims that the shapes on the rock occurred from scarring battles between the snake gods Kuniya and Liru, and the actions of the hare-wallaby people, the Mala.*

ABOVE *The enigmatic dingoes are important ancestral beings in Aboriginal creation stories.*

OPPOSITE *The Ewaninga Rock carvings are very special and precious. Sadly, they were created so long ago that the meanings of the stories depicted have been forgotten.*

RIGHT *Standley Chasm is one of the most dramatic gaps in the MacDonnell Ranges. Only nine metres wide and soaring to a height of about 80 metres, the chasm walls burst into a fiery red as the sun arcs overhead at midday.*

BELOW & FOLLOWING PAGES *The awe-inspiring, massive domes of Katatjuta are cleaved by deep canyons and wide valleys where plants, animals and birds flourish.*

DIAMONDS & PEARLS

Broome and the Kimberley

There is no place in Australia that reveals the continent's size more than the rugged and largely impenetrable Kimberley region in the far north of Western Australia. Isolated cattle stations, averaging half-a-million hectares each, are spread over the savannah-covered plateaux. Hardy farmers round up cattle by helicopter, children study by tuning in to the School of the Air, and the local GP is the Flying Doctor.

The southern gateway to the Kimberley is the pearling port of Broome. At the turn of the century, hundreds of divers toiled out of Broome to reap most of the world's mother-of-pearl. The early influences of the Malays, Filipinos, Chinese and Japanese who emigrated to dive the fields can be seen in the red-trimmed houses and pagoda-topped telephone booths.

Today, Broome is the centre of thriving cultured pearl, cattle-rearing and tourist industries. Wonderful shell-collecting beaches lie near the city and camel trains give visitors a lift along the popular Cable Beach.

A staggering 3229 kilometres from Perth lies the northernmost town and major port of Wyndham, where tourists come to spot crocodiles basking in their natural habitat, peer at ancient Aboriginal rock paintings, and visit the boab Prison Tree, estimated to be 4000 years old.

Close by Wyndham is Kununurra, the major centre for the largest diamond mine in the world, the Argyle. Nearby, the Ord River Project now irrigates previously infertile lands to produce a feast of melons, bananas, sunflowers, maize, peanuts, soya beans, and hay. The Ord River offers the best barramundi fishing in Australia.

Halls Creek, site of the first gold rush in Western Australia, is also near the site of the second-largest meteorite crater in the world, while the Purnululu (Bungle Bungle) National Park displays unique fan palms that cling to near-vertical, 200-metre-high, striped sandstone domes.

ABOVE *Pearling luggers have been operating out of Broome since the 1880s, combing fields where mother-of-pearl is still harvested. But Broome's cultured pearls industry is what has made the town world famous. The Shinju Matsuri (Festival of the Pearl) is celebrated annually in August or September.*

OPPOSITE *Buccaneer Rock at Roebuck Bay was named after the ship of William Dampier, an English pirate who first sighted this coast-line in 1699. It is estimated that around 800 000 wading birds flock to Roebuck Bay annually. Birdwatching tours and an observatory make this a nature lover's paradise.*

ABOVE *At low tide the 130 million-year-old dinosaur foot-prints at Gantheaume Point are visible. Impressions of the prints are set in concrete nearby.*

OPPOSITE LEFT *The cool pool at the Palm Resort, Cable Beach, offers a welcome respite after a day's sightseeing.*

OPPOSITE RIGHT *Seeded oyster shells at Willie Creek Pearl Farm allow visitors to see how a precious pearl is created.*

RIGHT *A sunset saunter on a camel across the sands at Cable Beach is a romantic and memorable way to end the day.*

ABOVE & RIGHT *The spectacular beehive-shaped domes in the Purnululu (Bungle Bungle) National Park are coated with stripes of black lichen and orange silica.*

OPPOSITE *Windjana Gorge National Park is an ancient limestone reef, forged over the millennia by the Lennard River.*

BELOW *When the Fitzroy River floods, it rises 16 metres and scours the cliffs of Geikie Gorge.*

BOTTOM *The Prison Tree is a large hollow boab that was once used to lock up the famous rebel, Jandamarra.*

TOP & ABOVE *The Argyle Homestead Museum at Kununurra is a reconstruction of the Durack family homestead, which was dismantled when the Ord River was dammed. The museum provides a unique insight into the lives of one of the most famous and hardy pioneering families in Australia.*

RIGHT *Lake Argyle, containing nine times the volume of water in Sydney Harbour, is the result of the damming of the Ord River. Camping, boating and fishing for barramundi are major drawcards to this expansive lake. Close by are the rugged hills, deep valleys and gorges of the spectacular Mirima (Hidden Valley) National Park.*

OPPOSITE & BELOW *Stretching for kilometres and looking like a miniature version of its namesake, the China Wall at Halls Creek forms a vein of loops around the countryside. It is thought to be a section of a single fault, the largest of its type known in the world.*

ABOVE, LEFT & RIGHT *The first gold rush in Western Australia occurred at Halls Creek in 1885. Halls Creek is now the centre of a thriving beef industry. However, the crumbling relics of cars and the walls of the mud-built post office still tell tales of a different time.*

RICHES OF THE WEST

Perth, Rottnest Island and Shark Bay

estern Australia – comprising almost a third of the continent – is as the early explorers noted, daunting. But, in stark contrast to the harshness of the north and the largely inhospitable, hot inland deserts, the mid-west and south-western regions are places of great fertile charm.

The state capital, Perth, is located on the Swan River 20 kilometres upriver from Fremantle's port. Eighty per cent of the state's 1.8 million people live here where they enjoy an easygoing, outdoor lifestyle.

Perth is renowned for its almost endless blue skies, parks and gardens, turn-of-the-century buildings and modern sky-scrapers, and more boat and yacht clubs per capita than any other city in the world.

There are 10 national parks within a 100-kilometre radius of the city. In spring vast areas ignite, almost overnight, in a blaze of colour as more than 10 000 species of wildflower come to life. Many sprout in the undergrowth of the soaring jarrahs and massive million-year-old karri trees. Over 90 bird species are attracted to these feasts of nectar, from the 2-metre-tall emus to tiny 15-centimetre emu wrens, high-flying sea eagles, kites, purple-crowned lorikeets and white-tailed black cockatoos.

Just offshore from Perth is a favourite weekend getaway for the city's residents. Rottnest Island in the Indian Ocean is a tranquil haven where no cars are allowed. North of Perth lies Shark Bay, where dolphins come ashore to be fed daily and green turtles, dugongs and ospreys feed in shallow seagrass beds. At Ningaloo Reef snorkellers can view an endless parade of brilliant tropical fish, manta rays, and the timid, 12-metre-long, plankton-eating giant whale shark. Nearby the mysterious stromatolites join the list of strange and weird shapes, including the Pinnacles and Wave Rock, that make the state such an amazing place to explore.

ABOVE *Perched high on one of the few hills in Perth is the gracious St Mary's Cathedral. Built in 1865, just 35 years after the founding of the city, the church was remodelled in 1929 and is set in a large, rambling garden that recalls the early days of the colony.*

OPPOSITE
Situated between the sparkling water of the Indian Ocean and the green hills of the Darling Range, Perth sits majestically on the widest part of the Swan River. Today's cosmopolitan city was built on the wealth of Western Australia's vast diamond, gold, mineral and agricultural industries.

LEFT *The striking Burswood Casino entices both the high-rollers and occasional flutterers to its baize-topped tables and poker machines.*

BELOW *South Terrace in Fremantle is a great place for coffee, gelato, or simply watching the passing parade of people from the outdoor cafe tables.*

OPPOSITE *The majestic and inspirational University of Western Australia was built of limestone quarried from the ground it now stands upon.*

BELOW *Built in 1830, the Round House in Fremantle was the first gaol of the Swan River Colony and is the oldest public building in Western Australia.*

ABOVE *As no cars are permitted on peaceful Rottnest Island, cycling on land or water is a means of getting around. Thomson Bay also offers a fabulous fishing location.*

LEFT *The idyllic island has attracted watersport enthusiasts for generations. Snorkellers revel in the crystal-clear waters near the Bathurst Lighthouse.*

BELOW *Dutch explorer, Willem de Vlamingh, thought the quokka was a large rat and so named the island 'Rat's Nest', from which Rottnest was adopted. The quokka is in fact a tiny, gregarious marsupial.*

ABOVE *Monkey Mia at Shark Bay is a favourite fishing ground for both dedicated fishermen and pelicans.*

RIGHT *Hamelin Pool is home to these stromatolites, meaning 'stony carpet' in Greek. Relics from the prehistoric era, they are formed, layer upon layer, by microscopic blue-green algae which trap bits of sediment.*

BELOW *Monkey Mia is also famous for its curious bottlenose dolphins which come close to shore to commune with humans.*

ABOVE & LEFT *Nambung National Park attracts visitors who come to stare in awe at the strange Pinnacles. These limestone formations can be up to four metres tall.*

OPPOSITE *Wave Rock is an ancient granite outcrop that curves 15 metres into the air. Close by are other fascinating rock formations like Hippo's Yawn, Breakers and The Humps.*

BELOW *The thorny devil is covered in sharp spikes and survives by collecting moisture in the channels on its skin.*

ABOVE *One of Australia's best-known and best-loved animals, the kangaroo, enjoys Western Australia's abundance of wildflowers as much as the tourists.*

SOUTHERN SPOILS

Adelaide, Barossa Valley and Kangaroo Island

With a Mediterranean climate and extraordinary landscapes, South Australia is a captivating state. This city of churches competes for attention with vineyards that stretch across undulating hills, and an island where the flora and fauna have continued to flourish peacefully away from mainland predators for centuries.

The Torrens River, lined with grassy banks, shady gums and willows, drifts through the wide open parks and gardens of Adelaide. Broad, tree-lined streets laid out in symmetrical, square-mile grids run between elegant historic buildings and numerous churches. Designed by Colonel William Light for the wealthy settlers who arrived on these shores in 1836, today it is Australia's fourth-largest city, with a population of over a million. Adelaide bustles with sidewalk cafes, outdoor pedestrian malls, street markets and popular beaches like Glenelg.

A short drive from the city lie the gentle mountains and fertile farmlands of the Adelaide Hills. The nostalgically restored village of Hahndorf is the site of the oldest-surviving German settlement in Australia. Nearby, conservation parks and forests provide close-up views of parrots, galahs, honey-eaters, emus, kangaroos and wallabies.

North and south of Adelaide are South Australia's fabled wine regions. The most widely known is the Barossa Valley with over 50 wineries open to the public, and year-round festivals to celebrate the ambrosial harvest.

Kangaroo Island, 145 kilometres long and 60 kilometres wide, lies at the entrance to the Gulf St Vincent. Dense and diverse vegetation, plus the absence of predators, provide a haven for koalas, emus, platypus, the small tammar wallaby and, obviously, the kangaroo. Pelicans and sea eagles flock to the island's coastline as do seals, sea lions and penguins, while the crystalline waters attract scuba divers, snorkellers and fishermen.

ABOVE *Quiet, manicured lawns enhance the beauty of the Torrens Rivers as it winds its way through Adelaide. This tranquil waterway is surrounded by a number of sights, including the Festival Centre, the Zoological Gardens, The University of Adelaide and the Adelaide Oval.*

OPPOSITE *Adelaide's St Peter's Cathedral was constructed between 1860 and 1904. It was designed by the notable English architect, William Butterfield, who also designed St Paul's in Melbourne.*

ABOVE *The Adelaide Botanic Gardens' Bicentennial Conservatory is the largest in the Southern Hemisphere and houses a breathtaking tropical rainforest.*

LEFT *As rowers tackle the Torrens River, its shimmering depths capture the image of the city's skyscrapers.*

BELOW & BOTTOM *To enjoy a stroll along the shore and pier at Glenelg, a beachside suburb, catch the vintage 1929 Bay Tram which departs from the city centre.*

101

OPPOSITE TOP *As the sun rises over the Barossa Valley, it is not hard to see why German settlers in 1842 realised the potential of the region and planted the crops that created an economic boost for the state.*

RIGHT *Picturesque villages and home-steads, some with marble buildings and deep cellars, separate the vast regular rows of vines from each other.*

BELOW *The extensive Barossa Valley vineyards account for a quarter of all Australia's wine production.*

ABOVE *Recalling the grand chateaus of France, Chateau Yaldara has high ceilings, polished floorboards and beautiful furnishings.*

OPPOSITE *Some of the older wineries in the Barossa, like Chateau Yaldara, capitalise on the charm of another era and open their doors to the public.*

RIGHT *The Herbig Tree in Springton is an enormous, hollow red gum that became the home of the pioneering Herbig family between 1855–1860. Photographs of the family living in the tree are on display along with other pioneer relics.*

BELOW *Springton is north-east of Adelaide and its attractive countryside supports a thriving mohair industry.*

ABOVE *Kangaroo Island's Remarkable Rocks have been hollowed out by the weather over millions of years. These huge boulders sit precariously balanced on a huge dome of granite, 75 metres above the surging sea.*

OPPOSITE BOTTOM *New Zealand fur seals come ashore to play at Seal Bay on Kangaroo Island. They have become so accustomed to people that it is possible to walk amongst them.*

RIGHT *Kangaroo Island provides endless opportunities to meet native wildlife such as the appealing koala.*

OPPOSITE *Kangaroo Island's Kelly Hill Caves are spectacular glistening limestone formations. They were discovered when a stockman and his horse, Kelly, slipped into a sinkhole.*

BELOW *Not far from the main centre on the island, Kingscote, the cliffs gradually descend to sea level at a place known as The Bluff.*

ABOVE *At Weirs Cove are the remains of a storehouse, where material had to be hauled up the precipitous cliff by flying fox in order to build the lighthouse at Cape du Couedic.*

BELOW *From Harveys Return near Cape Borda, the northern cliffs of the island extend around to the Western River Conservation Park.*

SCENIC WEALTH

Melbourne, the Great Ocean Road and Phillip Island

Victoria's spectacular coastline, picturesque national parks and graceful cities provide continual enticement. Tales of rich pastures similar to those in England brought a rush of settlers in the early 1800s. Those pioneers were followed by fortune-seekers to the goldfields in the north. The early economic boom can be seen in the capital's gracious buildings, but a host of natural panoramas swell the allure of the Garden State.

Australia's second-largest city with a population of over three million, Melbourne is set against the tree-clad, picturesque Dandenong Ranges and covers more than 1300 square kilometres. The Yarra River loops through its elegant suburbs and under ornate Victorian bridges before entering the deep-water port of Port Phillip Bay.

Melbourne's graceful Victorian architecture, chic shopping arcades and pre-eminence as the cultural centre of Australia sets the city apart from any other. Its cosmopolitan make-up is apparent in the festive multicultural events and the wide variety of cuisine. Melbourne people are also sports crazy and play host to events such as the Australian Open Tennis Championships, the Australian Grand Prix, the Melbourne Cup, and Australian Rules Football, teasingly referred to as the state's religion.

To the west, the winding Great Ocean Road runs past seaside towns, forests and lighthouses, as well as rugged landforms carved by the mighty Southern Ocean. The 400-kilometre drive follows the contours of the coastline from Geelong to the South Australian border and provides some of the world's most spectacular coastal scenery.

Phillip Island is renowned for its beauty and wildlife. A must is the parade of penguins who waddle to their burrows on the beach each night, but other big drawcards include its beaches, wildlife, watersport facilities, quiet walking tracks and the annual 500cc Racing Grand Prix.

ABOVE *Melbourne continues to buzz right through the night. Along the shores of the Yarra are fine restaurants, entertainment venues and magical walkways. The city is easily navigable, right up to the Dandenongs in the distance, by its rectangular grid of wide avenues and roads with interconnecting arcades and alleys.*

OPPOSITE *The impressive Governor's Mansion sits on the fringe of one of the finest botanical gardens in the world. Combined with imposing high-Victorian architecture and more parks than any other city in Australia, Melbourne balances a passion for the present with the past.*

ABOVE *Flinders Street Station is one of Melbourne's well-known landmarks. Built in 1854, it is the oldest metropolitan railway station in Australia.*

OPPOSITE *The Victorian Arts Centre showcases innovative exhibitions, stages concerts and plays, and is the venue for a popular Sunday market.*

BELOW *Numerous food markets cater for shoppers and restaurateurs. Victoria Markets is a Melbourne institution.*

ABOVE *Pollution-free electric trams link the city centre to the outlying suburbs. Colourfully painted by artists, many resemble mobile murals.*

BELOW *The promenade at Southgate bustles with entertainment and an extraordinary range of shops and eateries.*

ABOVE *The Australian Grand Prix is one of many international sporting events which have brought Melbourne to the world's television screens.*

LEFT *The heritage-classified Old Melbourne Gaol, where notorious Ned Kelly was hanged, is now a museum.*

OPPOSITE *Port Phillip Bay is lined with 97 kilometres of broad, popular beaches.*

BELOW *On the first Tuesday in November the nation stops to watch the Melbourne Cup, undoubtedly the highlight of the racing year.*

OPPOSITE *Cliff-edge walking tracks provide spectacular views of the coastal and offshore stacks of majestic limestone formations, including the Twelve Apostles and Loch Ard Gorge at Port Campbell National Park.*

ABOVE & BELOW *The surging seas along the southern coast have caused a number of shipwrecks. In 1878, the iron clipper,* Loch Ard, *went down with only two survivors. A plaque atop the gorge named after the vessel recalls the event.*

ABOVE *Built by returned soldiers as a memorial to their fallen comrades in World War I, the Great Ocean Road hugs a winding coastline of dramatic scenery.*

RIGHT *Port Fairy, at the mouth of the Moyne River, is home to a fishing fleet which returns each evening with catches of crayfish and abalone. Whale spotting along this coastline draws thousands of spectators every year.*

BELOW *Warrnambool, located towards the end of the Great Ocean Road, was once a major shipping port but its harbour is too shallow for modern ships. One of the city's most popular attractions is Flagstaff Hill, a recreation of the maritime village.*

RIGHT *Thousands of visitors flock to Summerland Beach on Phillip Island each afternoon to watch some 2000 tiny penguins waddle to their burrows at sunset.*

OPPOSITE *Fishermen compete with pelicans, swans, gulls, spoonbills and eagles for the spoils of the ocean at Newhaven on the mouth of Westernport Bay.*

BELOW *The Nobbies on Phillip Island are famous rock formations that have a wild and rugged beauty.*

NATIONAL SHOWPIECE

Canberra and the Snowy Mountains

With Parliament House and its 81-metre-high flagpole on Capital Hill at its centre, Canberra's unique circular streets and grand avenues radiate through vast parklands towards the outer suburbs in the surrounding hills and mountains.

In 1901, six colonies united to form the Commonwealth of Australia. An intense rivalry grew between Sydney and Melbourne as to which city would be the capital until, after much debate, 2330 hectares of sheep-grazing land on the Murrumbidgee River was purchased in 1908. The land became the Australian Capital Territory, and Canberra – from the Aboriginal word *kamberra* for 'meeting place' – the nation's capital.

Canberra is a city from the drawing board of Walter Burley Griffin, a Chicago-born architect. Lake Burley Griffin, created by damming the Molonglo River, is the city's water playground. The soaring 53-bell carillon, 150-metre spray of the Captain Cook Memorial Water Jet, and 35 kilometres of parks along the shoreline provide spectacular back-drops to the rowboats, yachts and ferries that thread its gentle waters.

The real treasures of Canberra, though, are its stunning architecture and indoor wonders. There's the beautiful 20-metre-long Arthur Boyd tapestry inside the lawn-topped Parliament House, the stained-glass windows of the National Library, and the Aboriginal artefacts housed in the National Gallery of Australia. The copper-domed Australian War Memorial recalls the valour of Australian soldiers in nine wars, while the Australian Institute of Sport has the very latest facilities to assist the country's sporting heroes.

Canberra is only 170 kilometres from the Snowy Mountains and the Kosciusko National Park. In summer, trout fishing in mountain streams and walks through giant mountain ash and luxuriant fern gullies are a must; while in winter, vast snowfields are a hub of activities.

ABOVE *Magnificent public buildings, housing some of Australia's most priceless art, pale in comparison to Parliament House, atop Capital Hill. Its unique shape reflects Canberra's position as the nucleus of Australian politics. The elegant city is host to over 60 diplomatic missions.*

OPPOSITE *An entire hilltop was carved away to build Parliament House. When the building was completed, the dirt was put back and grass was grown on the roof around the tall, stainless-steel flagpole. Australians humorously comment that this is the only place where the public can walk over their politicians.*

OPPOSITE *The old Parliament House was opened by the Duke of York (later King George VI) in 1927. It remained the seat of government until 1988. The National Portrait Gallery is now housed behind the elegant lines of its symmetrical facade.*

BELOW *The 195-metre-high Telstra Tower provides panoramic views of the award-winning public buildings studded around Lake Burley Griffin. Unlike the state capitals, Canberra is located inland, enjoying a continental climate with four distinct seasons.*

ABOVE *Walter Bunning designed the National Library with a Greek temple in mind. The library contains collections of paintings, rare manuscripts and film archives.*

ABOVE *In spring, Canberra celebrates with its annual Floriade festival, showing off its striking floral displays with music, dance and theatrical events.*

LEFT *Stained-glass windows in the Australian War Memorial, along with the Tomb of the Unknown Australian Soldier, commemorate Australia's fine record of military involvement.*

OPPOSITE *Cockington Green in Canberra is a model of the English village in Devon of the same name. It reminds visitors of Australia's ties to its mother country.*

ABOVE, TOP & LEFT *The highest mountains in Australia lie at the southern end of the vast 690 000-hectare Kosciusko National Park. The greatest of these are the Snowy Mountains where thousands come to ski, snowboard and have fun on the slopes in winter, and to partake in its varied and active après-ski activities. There are several world-class resorts, some with heart-stopping downhill courses and others leading to cross-country trails which are among the best in the world. The largest of the ski fields is Perisher Blue, comprising 1605 hectares. The twisting and gravity-defying tricks at the spotlighted Aerial Night Spectacular are just one of Perisher's many thrilling attractions.*

ABOVE *In summer at Lake Jindabyne, on the edge of Kosciusko National Park, boats and waterskiers part its tranquil surface while fishermen are lured by brown and rainbow trout in the lake and nearby streams.*

RIGHT *Alternately placid and wild, rivers flow through the ruggedly beautiful terrain of Kosciusko National Park where bushwalkers and campers follow countless trails to exhilarating views of alpine lakes and wooded valleys.*

BELOW *A natural wonderland, vivid wildflowers carpet the slopes and plains of Kosciusko National Park while kestrels and falcons soar above the valleys. Kangaroos and wallabies graze on the pastures, while crimson rosellas, cockatoos and flame-breasted robins flit between giant mountain ash and luscious ferns.*

EMERALD ISLAND

Hobart and Tasmania

Abel Tasman first sighted this unique island in 1642. At first, it was thought to be part of the mainland and so remained largely ignored until Governor King proclaimed its British sovereignty in 1803. Settlers soon arrived, attracted by rich pastures and free labour from the island's newly established penal colony. The convicts were treated brutally, but their legacy remains in numerous bridges and graceful buildings, and the sandstone ruins of the Port Arthur penal settlement.

Lying 24 kilometres south of Victoria and covering an area just over half the size of England, the land that once struck dread into the hearts of convicts now beckons the adventurer.

Hobart, the capital and home to 133 000 people, is located on the panoramic Derwent River. With its well-preserved colonial buildings and spectacular, deep-water harbour, Hobart certainly does enchant. From the docks you can watch the finish of the Sydney to Hobart Ocean Yacht Race or the Royal Hobart Regatta. In narrow, winding streets at Battery Point and in converted sandstone warehouses at Salamanca Place, galleries and eateries abound. The first casino in Australia was built in Tasmania and is positioned on the water's edge.

Reminiscent of the English countryside, the state's fertile hedgerowed fields yield abundant harvests of apples, strawberries, grapes, hops, and potatoes and burst into colour with pure lavender harvests and the only legally grown poppies in the world.

Fourteen national parks have preserved the true character of Tasmania's wilderness of jagged mountains, densely forested valleys, glacial lakes and cascading waterfalls. Savage rivers beckon white-water rafters, and over 3000 lakes offer some of the best trout fishing in the world. Giant gum trees, Antarctic beech and Huon pines compete for attention with rare orchids, Tasmanian devils, orange-bellied parrots and native black currawong.

ABOVE *The first casino in Australia, the circular Wrest Point Federal Casino, towers tall amid more than 90 heritage-listed buildings in Hobart. While the city has changed little from the days when whalers and sealers thronged to its taverns, today dozens of pubs and restaurants offer the finest in food and wine.*

OPPOSITE *Mount Wellington, 1270 metres high, offers a great vantage point from which to view Hobart with its magnificent deep-water port and spread of waterways. Extending on both banks of the Derwent River, the city is renowned for its amiable atmosphere, friendly citizens and historic attractions.*

ABOVE *Salamanca Place with its backdrop of carefully restored sandstone warehouses draws the crowds each weekend to hunt for bargains at the market stalls.*

OPPOSITE *The Tasman Bridge joins Hobart's eastern suburbs to the city centre. The Royal Tasmanian Botanical Gardens on the city side of the bridge are renowned for their floral displays, Mount Fuji replica and extensive variety of plants.*

RIGHT *Constitution Dock marks the end of the Sydney to Hobart Ocean Yacht Race and signals the start of week-long victory celebrations.*

ABOVE *Port Arthur is Australia's most significant historical site. Despite its tranquil exterior, between 1830 and 1877 around 12 500 convicts passed through the settlement where they were subjected to brutal treatment.*

RIGHT *The Richmond Bridge, the oldest in Australia, was built by convicts and spans the Coal River. The perfectly preserved, colonial village of Richmond is nearby.*

BELOW *The Penitentiary at Port Arthur was once a convict-powered mill and still stands as a relic of Tasmania's penal settlement. The nightly 'Ghost Tour' conducted at the ruins recalls the area's shadowy past.*

ABOVE *Cradle Mountain–Lake St Clair National Park is famous for the stark grandeur of its glacial lakes, rugged mountains, forests and waterfalls.*

LEFT *The lavender fields at Nabowla produce the purest strains in the world. Originally transported to Tasmania in 1922, the stock has never been cross-pollinated.*

BELOW *This wallaby is one of the many animals that has learnt to adapt to Tasmania's often freezing winters.*

ABOVE *Tasmania is crossed by many wild rivers and tempts the adventurous with its white-water rafting courses.*

BELOW AND OPPOSITE *Freycinet National Park is renowned for its pink granite cliffs, clear waters, unspoilt beaches and forested coastline.*

ABOVE *Tasmania's isolation and its protected parks have ensured the survival of the Tasmanian devil, which is now extinct on the mainland.*

FOLLOWING PAGES *Serene Lake Sorell in the central highlands offers some of the best trout-fishing waters in the state.*

INDEX